PTS. - 0.5

A New True Book

MOUNTAINS

By Lynn M. Stone

This "true book" was prepared
under the direction of
Illa Podendorf,
formerly with the Laboratory School,
University of Chicago

CP CHILDRENS PRESS, CHICAGO

Medicine Bow Peak, Snowy Range, Wyoming

PHOTO CREDITS

Jerry Hennen—Cover, 2, 4 (top), 11 (top right), 16 (2 photos), 18 (3 photos), 20, 21, 27 (top left), 31 (right), 32 (left), 38 (left), 45

Jerome Wyckoff—23 (top left)

Lynn M. Stone—4 (bottom), 15 (2 photos), 17 (left), 23 (right and bottom left), 25 (left), 27 (top right, bottom left), 29 (2 photos), 30 (2 photos), 31 (left), 34 (2 photos), 36 (top), 37, 38 (right), 41, 43

James M. Mejuto—17 (right)

Root Resources: ©Lia Munson, 11 (bottom); ©Earl L. Kubis, 12; ©Ted Farrington, 32 (right)

James P. Rowan—8 (top), 11 (top left), 36 (bottom)

Marty Hansen—39

Mark Rosenthal—25 (right), 40 (2 photos)

Chandler Forman—8 (bottom left)

Lorraine Matys—8 (bottom right)

Louise Lunak—14

Hillstrom Stock Photos—©Vic Banks, 33 (left); ©Tom J. Ulrich, 33 (right); ©Jessie Walker, 6

COVER—Maroon Bells, Colorado

For my mother and father who
encouraged my sense of direction

Library of Congress Cataloging in Publication Data

Stone, Lynn M.
  Mountains.

  (A New true book)
  Includes index.
  Summary: Briefly describes mountains and the plants, animals, and people that live in mountainous areas.
    1. Mountain ecology—Juvenile literature.
  2. Mountains—Juvenile literature. [1. Mountain ecology.
  2. Mountains. 3. Ecology] I. Title.
  QH541.5.M65S76 1983   574.5′264   83-7276
  ISBN 0-516-01698-9   AACR2

TABLE OF CONTENTS

Payto Lake, Canadian Rockies

Hurricane Ridge, Olympic National Park

WHAT IS A MOUNTAIN?

This is a mountain. As you can see it rises much higher than the other land around it.

Mountains are higher than hills. Mountains usually have steep sides. Their sides and tops, or peaks, are often rocky.

Mountains can cover huge areas of land. They are found in groups called ranges. A range can be from several miles to hundreds of miles long.

A mountain is measured by how high it is above the ocean or sea level. The highest mountains are in Asia.

Kanchenjunga, elevation 28,146 feet, in the Himalaya Mountains in Asia.

The highest mountain of all is Mount Everest. It stands five and one-half miles above the ocean!

Mountains were formed long, long ago by very strong movements under the ground. The force of these movements pushed earth and rocks upward.

Top: Longs Peak, elevation 14,255 feet,
in the Rocky Mountains
Above left: Ruins of the Inca Indians of Peru
were discovered high in the Andes Mountains
Right: Cinder cones at Haleakala (House of the Sun)
on the island of Maui, Hawaii. Cinder cones form in
the craters of volcanoes.

Mountains rise on every continent. The longest range in the world is the Andes of South America. The longest range in North America is the Rocky Mountains. Mount Everest is part of the Himalayas, a range in Asia.

Mountains rise from deserts, plains, forests, and even oceans. The Hawaiian Islands are tops of a range of underwater mountains.

ALL MOUNTAINS ARE NOT ALIKE

All mountains are not alike. Some are worn by ice, wind, and rain. These older mountains have more rounded tops than newer mountains. The Appalachian Mountains of the eastern United States are old, worn mountains. Newer mountains, like the Tetons, often have sharp, rocky tops.

Cumberland Mountains (above) and the Great Smoky Mountains (left) are part of the Appalachian Mountains. The Tetons (below) are part of the newer Rocky Mountains. Lower, older mountains, like the Appalachians, can be almost covered with trees.

Some mountains are much taller than others. Mount Kilimanjaro in East Africa and Mount McKinley in North America are always snowcapped.

Zebras graze on the plains near Mount Kilimanjaro, elevation 19,321 feet.

MOUNTAIN PLANTS

Many kinds of plants
grow on mountains.

Near the bottom of
mountains grow plants and
trees that need warmth.
Fewer and smaller plants
grow in the higher, colder
parts of mountains.

Mountains in warm
climates have different
kinds of plants than
mountains in cold climates.

Volcanic mountains in French Polynesia in the South Pacific

Mountains with heavy rains grow different plants than dry mountains.

Mountains in very warm countries have cloud forests and rain forests. Only plants that need large amounts of water can grow there.

Redwood forests in California

The Coast Range in northern California rises by the Pacific Ocean. Rainfall there is heavy. The tallest trees in the world grow there! They are the redwood trees.

Mountain ranges with less rain have other kinds of plants. The Appalachians have many trees with wide green leaves. In autumn the leaves die. The tree branches are bare in winter. Many mountains have evergreen trees. They are green all year long.

Evergreens (left) are green all year long. The leaves of many trees in the White Mountains (right) change color in autumn.

Bamboo trees   **Saguaro cactus**

Bamboo trees grow on the lower mountainsides in some parts of China.

Huge saguaro cactus plants—as large as trees— grow on the sides of dry mountains in southern Arizona.

17

Mountain meadow (above) in Montana. Timber line in Colorado (below left) and alpine tundra (below right) in Glacier National Park.

On the highest parts of most mountains, trees cannot grow. The place on a mountain where the trees stop growing is the timber line.

Many mountains have meadows and grassy parks. High meadows may be covered by a soft carpet of tiny plants. This carpet is called alpine tundra.

MOUNTAIN FEATURES

Mountains in cold places like Alaska have glaciers. Glaciers are huge masses of ice and snow. They are usually on mountainsides and in mountain valleys.

Athabaska Glacier in Alberta, Canada

Many streams start from snow melting in the mountains. Streams that tumble down mountains have waterfalls.

Part of a glacier melts in summer. The water flows into lakes and streams.

Snow, rock, and mud also may fall down a mountain. Such a fall is called an avalanche.

PEOPLE
IN THE MOUNTAINS

Mountains are too steep for many cities and roads to be built on them. It is hard to farm on mountains. It is hard to go from place to place in mountains. But people do live on mountains.

People use mountains for many things. They cut trees for firewood and homes. They raise cows,

Mountain valley in Norway.
The alpaca (above) and
the llama (left) grow
thick, warm coats of hair.
People use the hair
for weaving fabric
to make their
winter coats.

sheep, and goats in
mountain meadows.

In the Andes Mountains
people raise alpacas and
llamas.

Mountain people may work in mines. Miners find coal, silver, gold, copper, and other minerals in the mountains.

Mountains can be damaged by too much mining and woodcutting. The steep mountainsides are left bare. Wind, snow, and rain loosen the ground. Dirt and rocks begin to wash away.

In Europe many people live in the Alps and

Above: Quito, Ecuador, is in the Andes
Mountains.
Left: Halstadt, Austria, is a village in
the Alps.

Caucasus mountains. Some
North Americans live in the
Rockies and Appalachians.
Many people from Peru
and Bolivia live in the Andes.

La Paz, Bolivia, is the
highest capital city in the
world.

WILD ANIMALS
OF THE MOUNTAINS

Many mountain animals live by eating mountain plants. The little pika eats grass.

Pikas live high in the mountains of western North America.

Like rabbits, pikas dig an underground home called a burrow. They store great mounds of grass and live on the grass all winter.

The pika (above left), the golden mantled ground squirrel (above), and the olympic marmot live in burrows.

The furry ground squirrel also lives in a burrow. It sleeps there all winter.

The marmot is a big cousin to the ground squirrel.

The marmot eats grass and flowers and leaves. By fall it is fat and ready to sleep. It lives on its fat while it sleeps.

Some mountain animals have horns and four hard, sharp feet called hooves. The hooves of mountain goats and sheep are special. They help them keep their balance in steep places.

Above: Mountain goats
Left: Siberian ibex

The mountain goat of North America has short horns and a long, white coat. The ibex is a brown wild goat of Europe and Asia. It has long, curved horns.

29

Above: The yak is raised for its milk and meat.
Right: A male bighorn is called a ram.
It has thick, curled horns.

Mountain sheep in North America are called bighorns. Like mountain goats, the sheep eat plants.

The yak lives in the wild in some Asian mountains.

Mule deer (left) and elk (above)
come to the mountains in summer.

It is also raised for milk
and meat by some Asian
people.

Yaks, goats, and sheep
are always at home in
mountains. Deer and elk
are summer visitors. They

climb down to valleys and woodlands in winter.

Beavers live in mountain valleys. They use their sharp teeth to cut down trees. They block streams with the trees that they cut. The streams back up and make ponds.

Beaver dam (right) and two beavers at the entrance to their lodge (above).

The ptarmigan changes its colors in summer and winter. This makes it harder for its enemies to see it.

Many mountain birds are plant eaters. The ptarmigan is always looking for berries, twigs, and grass.

The ptarmigan has white feathers in winter. It has brown feathers in summer.

Blue grouse (above) and wild turkey (right)

The ptarmigan and blue grouse are cousins of chickens and turkeys. The blue grouse lives in western mountain forests in North America.

Wild turkeys live in the Appalachian Mountains.

MOUNTAIN HUNTERS

A few mountain animals must catch other animals to live. They are hunters with sharp claws. The animals they catch and eat are their prey.

Three of the biggest hunters are wild cats. The snow leopard lives high in the snowy Himalaya Mountains.

Siberian tigers are the largest cats in the world.

The snow leopard (right) lives in the Himalaya Mountains. The Siberian tiger (below) lives in the mountains of Russia and China.

Puma or mountain lion

They live in the mountains
of Russia and China.
The cougar or mountain
lion lives in North and
South America. Cougars
eat deer, rabbits, and other
small animals.
Bears live in mountains
of Asia, North America,

37

Black bear (above) and wolf (right)

South America, and Europe. Bears catch animals, but they also eat plants.

Wolves travel together in family groups called packs. Wolves live in a very few mountain ranges of Asia, Europe, and North America.

Golden eagle's eyes
are very powerful.
It can see small
animals from far away.
When it sees its
prey it dives
and captures it.

The golden eagle is a
hunting bird. It has a sharp,
hooked bill and sharp claws.
The golden eagle lives in
the mountains of Europe
and North America.

The California condor (above)
is almost as large as the
Andean condor (right). Almost all
the California condors are
gone now. People must help
them survive.

The Andean condor is
the largest flying bird in
the world. It lives in the
Andes Mountains. It usually
eats only dead animals.

The California condor is
smaller than the Andean bird.

Dusky salamander. Salamanders have wet, slippery bodies.

Salamanders are hunters, but they are only three or four inches long! They catch insects and other tiny animals.

Many salamanders live in the southern Appalachian Mountains. Many kinds that are found here live nowhere else in the world

Many fish spend their whole lives in mountain streams and lakes. Most mountain fish catch little animals like insects.

Snakes that live in mountains catch prey. The rattlesnake bites its prey. Its bite contains poison. Most mountain snakes bite, but most are not poisonous.

There are not as many hunting animals as there

Timber rattlesnakes are poisonous.

used to be. Some have been driven away by new towns and roads. Many have been killed for their fur, skins, and feathers. A few more have been killed because they ate farm animals.

ENJOYING MOUNTAINS

People like to camp, fish, ski, and hike in the mountains. They like to watch mountain animals.

People like to climb mountains. They often use special tools to help them climb. Mountains can be steep and slippery, cold and snowy. Mount Everest was climbed for the first time in 1953.

Tourists travel through the San Juan Mountains from Durango to Silverton on an old steam-powered train.

We should enjoy mountains and their plants and animals. We should help take care of them, too. Mountains are big and rugged, but they can be damaged if we are not careful with them.

WORDS YOU SHOULD KNOW

alpaca(al•PACK•ah)—a mammal of South America with long, silky hair which is used as wool for clothing

alpine tundra(AL•pyne•TUN•drah)—a large land area found in high mountains where mosses and small shrubs grow

antler(ANT•ler)—bony growths found on the heads of some animals that grow out each year and are shed at the end of a season

avalanche(AV•ah•lanch)—a large mass of snow, ice, earth, or rocks that falls or slides down a mountainside

burrow(BER•oh)—a hole, tunnel, or opening dug in the ground by a small animal

condor(KAHN•dor)—a very large bird that lives in the mountains of California and South America

continent(KAHN•tih•nent)—one of the seven large landmasses of the earth

glacier(GLAY•sher)—a large mass of ice and snow that moves very slowly down a valley or a mountainside

grouse(GROWSS)—a bird with a plump body and brownish or grayish feathers

huge(HYOOJ)—very, very large

ibex(EYE•bex)—a wild goat that lives in the mountains of Asia, Europe, and North Africa

llama(LAH•mah)—a mammal found in South America whose wool coat is used for clothing

marmot(MAR•mit)—a small burrowing animal with short legs and brownish fur

pika(PY•kah)—a small mammal related to a rabbit that lives in the mountains of the Northern Hemisphere

prey(PRAY)—an animal hunted or caught by other animals for food

ptarmigan(TAR•mih•jin)—a bird that lives in northern regions whose feathers are white in winter and brownish in summer

range(RAYNGE) — a group or a series of mountains

rugged(RUG • id) — having a rough, uneven surface

saguaro(sah • GWAH • roh) — a very large cactus with upward-
curving branches that grows in the southwestern United
States and Mexico

salamander(SAL • ah • man • der) — an amphibian

timber line(TIM • ber • LYNE) — the place on a mountain above
which trees do not grow

yak(YACK) — a mammal with long hair and horns found in the
mountains of central Asia

INDEX

About the Author

Lynn M. Stone was born and raised in Meriden, Connecticut. He received his undergraduate degree from Aurora College in Illinois and his master's degree from Northern Illinois University. Once a teacher in Sarasota, Florida, Mr. Stone currently teaches English to junior high school students in the West Aurora Public School system.

A freelance wildlife photographer and journalist, Lynn has had his work appear in many publications including National Wildlife, Ranger Rick, Oceans, Country Gentlemen, Animal Kingdom, *and* International Wildlife. *He has also contributed to Time-Life, National Geographic, Audubon Field Guide, and Hallmark Cards.*

Many of Lynn Stone's photographs have been used in the New True Books published by Childrens Press.